Petroglyph Beach

E. Russell Smith

Direct all enquiries to the publisher:
TheRightEyedDeer Press
PO Box 236
Haliburton, ON
Canada K0M 1S0
http://therighteyeddeer.weebly.com
ISBN 978-1-105-70990-6

Contents

The Eden Cycle

The Fern Island Cycle

The Cross-purposes Cycle

The One-on-One Cycle

The Circumnavigation Cycle

Publisher's Foreword

I met Russell about two years ago when he joined the online writing community, The Write Idea (www.helenwhittaker.net/phpBB2) . It didn't take very long for writers there to realise that he is an absolute gem of a poet.

He is many things : a gentleman, a scholar – of the world, words, people and place -- supportive of both the site and its competitions, along with his fellow writers.

Russell's poetry takes you right along with him on his many journeys. It teases you with myth, the complexity of the human condition, the simplicity of things that just are. Russell does it in such a way that he reveals himself to be no ethereal poet, no man aloof of others. He is just a man, extremely talented in the ways that he can relate what he sees and what he thinks.

When Russell approached me with the idea of publishing *Petroglyph Beach*, I was somewhat taken aback. As a small press, TheRightEyedDeer has published magazines and anthologies. We have talked about publishing a few books but no more than that. Suddenly, we have in our hands a collection of poetry from one of our most highly regarded poets. It is a daunting thing, this mission to produce and publish such a piece of finely crafted work, and to deliver and do it to the utmost of our abilities.

Russell's masterful writing in *Petroglyph Beach* will take you on a journey or two. It is a book that can be relished in one full sitting, or it can be nibbled in small delicious bites ... or both.

It is tricky to determine the cut-off point. To know when you have done all that you can to present a book from someone I consider amongst Canada's best poets. There is a time to say, 'This is good. It's time to print.'

And that time is now.

Enjoy.

Douglas Pugh, Editor
TheRightEyedDeer Press

Comments

This is a joy of a collection – lyrical, reflective, perceptive and so very readable. Throughout there is an overarching sense of place, as if the author is at one with its spirit, the essence of it, as if the places themselves has singled him out so that 'I am their part and partner ... I sing/of signs of weather and the times.'

These times are not only the present, however. This is a poet who bonds with the earth, with its rocks, its peoples, its histories and myths. A crumbling pier is not a ruin to be overlooked – it is part 'of a vanished bridge where early settlers crossed the creek' An ancient stone shaped like a bird has 'the sun/secreted under its wing'

The calm, quiet voice almost seems afraid that it may intrude upon or disturb the natural balance of the subject yet produces wonderful images and a power that seems to come from the landscape/timescape itself. This is truly a gift, beautifully, partially articulated in 'I and Thou Martin Buber' – 'My moment punctuates/the endless timescape./I am not defined... (but) catch /a transient glimpse beyond/ a brief reflection in the void./But snow will come again,/white, cold and carried/on the wind that even now/sighs through hemlocks/rising in the darkness.'
This is a book full of issues and questions – often understated and implicit but always there like an undercurrent in one of the rivers the poet journeys on. Read the poignant and disturbing Eden Cycle of poems and you'll see.

These are beautiful and important poems that deserve to be shared. The poet says it himself:

a night bird that sings briefly
and moves on
must be followed.

Mandy Pannett. Mike Noakes. (Poetry Editors 'The Right Eyed Deer)

'I have always enjoyed Russell's work. This collection certainly does not disappoint.'
- *John Unrau, Ontario.*

The
Eden
Cycle

The Summerhouse

A stream flowed out of Eden to water the garden....
Genesis 2:10

I paddle solo a backcountry river,
dark flat water flecked with spume
from a high cascade above, marbled
by the random eddies, clearing to reflect
a blue intenser than the sky itself,
and high white cumulus gleaming.
One red maple in the general green
portends the season's imminent change,

and under it, inverted also in the stream,
stands an old gazebo, only clue
that this is not a wilderness, although
throughout the whole long afternoon
I've been alone, down this slack reach
and one white spate that I must drag
to reach my launching site again.
How has it served, this edifice?

a trysting place, or else an Eden
for untroubled family gatherings,
where parents sat in friendly shade
on summer days long past, and watched
their naked children splash and shout,
swing and fall from the knotted rope
still hanging from a shoreline tree,
straight from green to glassy green.

Abdication

Sufficient unto the day is the evil thereof.
Matthew 6:34

Blue summer skies and velvet greens,
and later, on the table-top,
green baize — a brilliant evening
leads to justified repose and sleep,
innocent of license or neglect.

We were frugal in our middle years,
but now we take no thought for food,
or clothes, or shelter, asking only
whether Monday will be dry for golf,
or Tuesday balmy for the beach.

Our latest irritant may be
ahead of us, a laggard foursome
in the rough, a twosome driving
on the tee behind, an underbid
bridge contract going to slam.

Garnish for Cross Rib

Then God said, "Let us make man in our image, after our likeness."
Genesis 1:26

Rash faith is a savoury onion.
Peeling it raw reveals no core,
and yet, if left to thrive
it celebrates in pyrotechnic bloom,
sets its seed and multiplies.

I've spent my adult years
unlearning tales from childhood,
a well-done pabulum,
wisdom tastefully received
and braised with onion.

It says here that God
made Man in his own image —
a work in progress? Or
perhaps he abandoned the dish
when he overdid the sauce.

Gaia

The Lord God took the man and put him in the garden of Eden to till it and keep it.
Genesis 2:15

This afternoon a hundred crows
fly east, silent, except for yelling
"Hawk! " at a pair of circling red-tails.
There's been rain, and Sawmill Creek
is high, here where it enters the city,
before it's channeled, cribbed and curbed.

I push through shabby second growth,
tracing the line a king's surveyor
drew two centuries ago
with plane and alidade, and I
emerge (like him, I must suppose)
arrayed with burs and beggar-ticks.

Close to the Transpo overpass,
across the ravine from the railroad track
where the O-Train glides to town and back,
I sit in the sun on the crumbling pier
of a vanished bridge where early settlers
crossed the creek, and think I see

in craven crows and hungry hawks,
in streams confined in concrete walls,
in the craft of humankind arrayed
against the supple wilderness,
brief rivals only, in a neutral
cosmos that can never lose.

Flowers of Evil

Rachel is weeping for her children, because they are not.
Jeremiah 31:15

Before the rain, the hot wind
winnows birch chaff
over spiders' webs,
hairspun nets that camouflage
the dark intentions of the lily-beds.

After a late-day thunder shower
the sun returns to kindle
hanging drops of light
and to inflame the toxic fruit
that glows in guilty shadow.

July 18, 2006

[This month in Palestine the slaughter of innocents began another generation of hate.]

Last Skinny

"Behold, the man has become like one of us..."
Genesis 3:22

The convex lens
of the waxing quarter-moon
focuses the vagrant sun
(now below September's high perimeter),
gleaming on our knee-deep nakedness —

Eden to be locked in ice
with codes of access
we will recall when we return
from a season to the east
of icicles and winter twisters.

The Gospel According to Heidegger

The urban forest turns halfway
toward winter, here and there
a flare of fire in the green,

the seasonal effrontery
of heavy frost intruding
in the night's small hours.

A few brown flowers stand
another month in oblique sunlight,
omens to respect or overlook.

Such crises in the world set off
portentous bells at upper echelons —
in London, Tokyo and Washington.

The assurance of eventual death
and sheer oblivion makes us ask
if our existence has a point,

a holy grail, or if we should forego
this year's projected European tour.
We, however, keep our cool,

still certain of the infinite here,
the eternal now, and ergo, how
to stay the most alive in it.

West of Eden

"The voice of your brother's blood is crying to me from the ground..."
Genesis 4:10

We risk an unsafe footbridge to the yard,
over a slummy creek. Here died the days
of waney, stave and shingle, shaped by steam
till the boiler burst. The mill has burned, the
        stones
are overgrown, the shed and stable barred.
Along the river, wooden houses watch
like broody hens, guarding the jaded waste.
Close by, an empty highway sighs, and dies.

Out of the tangled wood, trembling aspens
enter the clearing. Boisterous jays and
        squirrels
poke and forage. Someone with a gun, a dog
and decoys watches from a tattered blind.
Another passes with a pack and bowl,
        prepared
to hunt and gather, looking to be spared.

Fort Needham Carillon

Remembering Halifax NS, December 6, 1917

Beeches lean away from the harbour,
brown leaves glowing in December sun.
Older than I, their limbs are pruned
low enough for a child to clamber in.
Thirteen bells recall that you stood here

one winter morning, looking west
as I do now, before the pylons, seeing
in the Narrows busy tugs and barges,
cranes, a floating drydock, cargo ships
and naval vessels moored or passing.

The SS Mont Blanc, loaded with munitions,
burning and abandoned, drifts against a pier,
and then, as Hell itself might gape, explodes.
Your last and lasting vision is a holocaust,
a preview of Hiroshima, that levels Halifax.

The harbour boils. The anchor flies and
falls beyond the city, where today it lies
beneath the shrouds of night and snow,
of dark and light, the cruel and merciful...
And you are either blind or dead.

Prufrock's Labyrinth

Long ago I saw a summit
far away and briefly clear,
and it became my lodestone.
Now, with every night's eclipse
I run into a wall of shadow

whether I have progressed
or not, and I retire to plead
that love song once again.
But morning always offers
some untested way to turn,

which I must follow, given
that my life goes on at all.
The new path rarely seems,
with my myopic vision,
to approach the goal.

Oh, do not ask, "What is it?"
How should I presume?
The daily despot points
to left, or right, or face-about,
and I proceed regardless.

Eden in Winter

The man called his wife's name Eve, because she was the mother of all living.
Genesis 3:20

In a downtown park I find
my marble Eve with broken hands and feet
lying awake by a sleeping man,
where he has carried her.

Unconscious, still he keeps her
among the frost-bit weeds,
a crippled captive
to oversee his wretchedness.

New life sings in the branches,
rattles the clinging leaves,
chases the hard snow crunching
sweet as halvah, beneath my feet.

Each lengthening day the sun
climbs higher over us.
I circle here; I listen
to her muted voice.

She tells me we are naked,
lacking even skins of animals,
and having eaten of the tree of life,
we could live forever.

Global Warning

And God said to them, "Be fruitful, and multiply,
and fill the earth and subdue it; and have dominion..."
Genesis 1:28
(So they did.)

Feeders filled with seed stay full
as weeks of February pass.
There's been so little snow that
finches find the thistles standing
high in fence rows, out beyond
the city boundary, and chickadees
are glad to hackle pine cones
or pick nutlets from the alders
growing out of naked stones.

Now, for slender comfort,
and only once each winter week,
a dark fly-past of carrion crows
escorts the trash collectors.
We have assumed dominion.
We devise our own extinction
while the singing birds survive
and thrive. We need them back
to animate our bitumen and brick.

Avuncular

Before I call her,
I walk in the park,
a narrow glassy footpath,
frigid wind, but a sun strong
and warm, open beechwoods
to penetrate, dreaming
old wilderness.

Before I call her,
I limp that country mile
of spring ice and frozen slush,
spasmodic hiccup of a winter
dying, east of Eden— a hard
mistake, on a heel bone
bruised by a fall.

When I do call,
her time is not her own;
she works the graveyard shift,
nine-day rotation, like myself
out of step with the world.

April for the Illegal

"The land is mine; with me you are but strangers and sojourners."
  Leviticus 25:23

By the patio, our sweet orange
(out of China) is in blossom and
in fruit, promise and reward together;
Arab hyacinths paint the terraces;
one solitary northern alien, a lilac
(once south Asian) glorious now
in purple sorrow, chosen for the stress
of summer heat and inferior winter.
Hummingbirds, migrating and ubiquitous,
twitter to and from a temporary nest —

High in the canyon, a small man
lurks and works in the shadow
of the sycamore and eucalyptus,
landless though the law provides
that in the seventh sabbath year
all land reverts to common tenure.
Still he hides and bides a bitter span,
raking trash for cash and secrecy.

Los Angeles, California

Coming to Jerusalem

"...every common bush afire with God:
But only he who sees takes off his shoes."
        E. B Browning, "Aurora Leigh" vii:810-811

Other pilgrims have stopped
out of weariness or sloth
or bad advice, and settled
for a fantasy, venerating
all the sainted dead enshrined
in holy reliquaries, giving up
on life before they die.

In this citadel at last, far from
the west side of the wilderness,
I stay my course to dance
barefoot on these cold stones.
Here I discover you once more,
my only burning bush.

Kingdom Come Saturday

"This shall be the first month of the year for you."
Exodus 12:2

Where are their palm leaves now?
Reporters mark a parabolic
falter in their fickle love
between Sunday's donkey ride
and the ninth hour yesterday.

Now they hear other voices,
cross the line from faith to madness.
Do not fret — lamb's blood is
on each doorpost and lintel.

Back to Eden

And the living creatures darted to and fro, like a flash of lightning.
Ezekiel 1:14

Too late for lies, fireflies
loosed from a plastic box
to fill the night, and though
we seize the flaming sword
and douse it, can we bribe
the fickle guardians? We can't
be sure of their corruption.
Nor can we see this garden
by our mortal lights.
We must invent new myths,
or find another oracle.

The
Fern Island
Cycle

Reaching Fern Island

The frozen bog shuts down for winter --
tamaracks and birches bare, black spruce
and white pine green along the ridge.
On the peat the heaths and laurels turn
to russet in the stooping sun. Ice needles
glaze the open water at the edge.
My territory, and I know it well —
the mire, the lagg, the sink-holes,
and a secret hummock with a fernery
of bracken, cinnamon and interrupted,
maidenhair, New York and ostrich,
polypody, oak and rattlesnake,
royal, sensitive and wood...

all ferns. I could take you there,
through speckled alder tangle and across
a beaver's ancient working, but I won't,
my acts being three ages, first
the seeker, asking what and why;
then, the mentor reaching back to help.
I've played those scenes, no longer
weigh the urgencies of younger players
waiting in the wings. Content to know
the little that I know, I cross the stage,
reciting rote soliloquies on the dozen
different native ferns that grow
on that small island in the mist.

Black Lace and Dandelion Wine

Staunch Methodist, Grandpa said
he took the pledge when he was twelve,
never to allow the demon drink

to pass his lips, swearing to eschew
John Barleycorn for ever.
His conviction didn't stretch

to new-decanted dandelion wine,
chilled and carried to his line
on hot midsummer mornings

by the widow on the quarter section
back of the alsike and timothy
where he was making hay.

Afternoons, Grandma brought him
oatmeal water, iced and salted —
never wearing black lace weeds.

Carrington, a Portrait

Remembering Dora Carrington 1893-1932

Left-handed, couldn't spell.
Paints, not words, her medium
for any surface — doors, walls
and furniture bore her landscapes,
figures, flowers and fantasies.

Men and women loved her,
in sustained succession.
She laid aside her brush
to give cold access
to her perfect body.

She kept her purest love
platonic, for one old bugger
who became infatuated
with all her passing men
in turn. When he died,

she took a shotgun to herself.
She bungled that as well,
suffering disemboweled
through hours of harrowing
to end her brush with life.

Embarkation

Here, through more than forty years,
we raised our children, and lived on.
Here their mother died, and here
I now have only space and things —
millstone, albatross, and anchor.

Here is the port of my departure,
where the young sailed long ago.
I'll go create new memories,
when I can jettison dead gods
of times and worlds now altered.

Et In Arcadia Ego

Rosa ranches in a canyon
of the thirsty chaparral.
Aurora's village lies between
the muskeg and the tamarack.
Neither takes to whisky.

For myself, I keep
in both their cupboards
a selected single malt,
aged ten-twelve years
in hand-picked oaks —

on one shelf, mellow Speyside
for the cool Pacific evenings;
on the other, Islay,
redolent
of peat fires and iodine,
for snowbound winter nights.

From the Grape-picker's Diary

Why, then comes in the sweet o' the year,
For the red blood reigns in the winter's pale.
The Winter's Tale IV.iii.3-4

A short October rain has passed
before mid-afternoon, and now
the sunken sun at supper time
spreads fiery ancient bloodlines
on the belly of the clouds.

The summer, past its equinox,
has lingered into long warm nights.
Now the vintner's lovely wife predicts
an arctic frost will come at dawn.
Tomorrow's skies will follow clear.

I'll pluck frozen Reisling and Vidal,
to be assured that sweet ice wines
may be at hand on long warm nights,
when the vintner's lovely wife and I
will make a winter's tale our own.

Farm Hands, Firm Hands

Every girlhood morning, every night
my mother's fists pulled milk
from Holstein cows, wrestled
reins and ploughs; they turned
the bedding and the butter churn.

They trained their grip
on dollars in the thirties,
held to a husband's arm
and wrists of children falling
into mud or into mischief.

Now they hold to life.
Her forearms firm,
those gentle hands
close on old years
slipping toward the century.

The Road to Merrickville

In memory of Eleanor Marritt Smith, 1903-2001

We have no reason now to drive
into the country south of Ottawa.
The land has taken her to itself,
after a pause for recollection
at the threshold of the dark.

Her last excursion out of doors
passed by a stone barn bridge,
solid as her father trading up and up,
her mother teaching her the ways
to make good times from hard.

Now, if we take that road, we see
old stone and even older timber
houses waiting for the rock and swale
to yield another crop. For centuries
an ageless forest saved this soil,

but after seasons of a settler's axe
and harrow, careless rain and snow-melt
leached and carried off the good of it.
She left her fields to fallow long ago.
Now strangers fill the land, content

with hobby horse and strolling green
around refurbished homesteads,
each one full of electronic toys
to make subsistence tolerable.
The world rolls east. The bright tide rises,

washes over relics wasted at the ebb,
and drives us up a steep defile.
Summer heat reflects in dry pools
on the road. The summit reached,
our weary mother stops a while.

She brought us here, and we go on.
She has stayed behind, content
to contemplate a promised land,
at last to take one easy step
alone, and in her own direction.

Dogs of the Mer Bleue

Clear sky, crisp air, and I ski
the Mer Bleue, first of the year
to break new snow, alone
with only the feral dogs.

I know how not to get lost
in a white-out. Follow the lagg,
hardwoods on one hand
black spruce bog on the other,

circle back over alien ground
minding the white pine horizon,
back-track a bitch that found
the path of least hostility

through tamarack and alder.
Muskrat huts are everywhere,
now the trappers have all gone
and left their dogs behind.

Newboro Lock

Sins of the fathers visit global heat
upon the children. Cicadas grieve.
One long note only, keen crescendo
and diminuendo lasting half a minute,
then decaying to exhausted silence.
Still the children shout and splash

from transom decks or cottage docks,
while I recline and watch the treetops
quiver in the heat. Two ancient maples
mingle branches in the easy air,
conspiring. Coupled crowns deprive
a neighbouring evergreen of light.

Blue jays, crows and cardinals
choose today to oust their adolescent young.
A red squirrel chatters to a juvenile
a diatribe on territory. Now the sun
declines at last into the cut. The locals
repossess the lake, the evening

stretching into endless possibilities,
one short darkness and a glassy dawn.
Before he leaves, the old lockmaster
tends his bedding plants, complaining
he has never had to stoop so low
to fill his watering can. I don't kneel

to pluck out weeds, or pray.
Standing up again can be too much.
My cooling system is inadequate.
I will sin again; the weeds will flourish.
Let them possess the perennial bed.
Time meets time at this high watershed.

Merryman's Yarn

She left O'Brian twice a widower,
once of a snake bite, so they say,
and that was on their wedding day.

Her angry bridegroom swore, b'gar,
there are no snakes in Ireland,
and she is mine, my morning star.

He would go to hell and back
to save her! This he tried, and failed,
searching the bottom of a whiskey jar.

And so, for him, she died again.
He lived out his redoubled pain, singing
songs to his guitar, to charming boys,

to bog birds, berry bush and rocks. At last,
when all his life was overcast, a court
of thwarted mistresses assaulted him.

More useless than a priest, they said.
He faltered, sloughed his human carapace
and settled in his spouse's resting place.

A Snowbird's Consolations

I miss the daily skate downtown,
and passionate skiing weekends.
Christmas is so white, but so is a beach
beside a green fairway, and I can play
on either one in summer shorts,
wander semi-naked in the semi-desert
through red-rose blooming ocotillas.
Here no sculptured ice on a frozen lake,
the signature of temporary winterlude;

sturdy bronze instead -- Cubist Lipschitz,
perforated Hepworth, Rubenesque Maillol
and malleable Moore, inverted in a pool
with lacy locusts and old acacias.
I walk at will, without my balaclava,
boots, mitts, scarf or overcoat, to scent
magnolias and flowering almonds,
weathering a short pink flurry, confetti
for an old affair that's now permissible.

Petals lie where they fall on patio stones
of havens and retirement homes,
pink or white or brown side up,
in random encounters, like dissidents
in Tahrir or Tiananmen, Times or Trafalgar,
fixed in a moment of waiting, waiting
for a shriving, for a shriveling,
for an acceptable number of deaths,
for the morning when the sweeper comes.

Los Angeles, February 2011

42

As Time Goes By

the scent of lilacs,
town parade,
boy on a pony
(someone's grandson),

tortillas, rellenos,
refried beans for lunch,
knees touching
under the table cloth,

delights we might have shared
when we were young
together,

as we are once more,
fifty years onward...

A Time to Heal

End of a day of sun and stony cold; I cross
the frozen marsh beyond Fern Island
and the end of ordinary tracks. New snow
flies beneath my skis. A dead pine   ·
scratches the twilight on the ridge,
Golgotha, after the Deposition.

Speckled alders thwart my access
to the lagg, my ice road to the acid bog.
The tundra needs a time away from me.
Her life has changed, a strange hand
rests on her perfect breast. Be patient
with her need for vigilant tranquility.

No one survives without a cicatrix
the traverse of a tangle such as this.
I can blame myself. I came to her
without an invitation, drawn by the spell
the arctic heath and laurel hold
for wanderers who chance upon her.

A Marriage at Pentecost

The priest stands apart in a woodland,
waiting with birdseed. The Spirit
descends like a chickadee
to his outstretched hand, charming
him in whom the Spirit is well pleased.

We bring our offering to be discovered
waiting in the marriage chamber
when the wild bird comes.
Daily we renew the provision.
After the bread and wine, the dance.

The
Cross-purposes
Cycle

Arm Ornament

"God sour the milk of the knacking wench "
Alden Nowlan, 1962

The winning candidate declaims
his fatuous victory speech
pausing frequently to let
the knackered multitude
admire him, smug and cute.
The plastic groupies cheer.

His porcelain plaything
clutches at his sleeve,
all bleach and cleavage,
naked thighs and nipples —
she looks on him adoringly.
Her cream is turning

but they suckle all the same,
enjoy the campaign smorgasbord
(it's what the party offers)
then withdraw the hand
that falls outside the covers
while they sleep between elections.

Foot Rules

A raven watchbird in the treetop croaks,
"Enter by the strait and lawful!
All who stray from the appointed path
will be indicted for no apparent reason."
A poet chasing an obscure afflatus
might bruise a blade of public grass.

And so we walk the designated course,
conform our pace to flags that strangers lay.
We don't allow that other feet might beat
a better way, nor suffer little ones
to trace their own green labyrinths
before the pavement is in place.

Footpaths evolve where walkers walk.
See! — someone has built a guilty crossing
at the brook — a dozen poles laid side by side
by children sneaking up Grasshopper Hill,
or dauntless birders with binoculars
spying out the wilderness beyond the pale.

Cross-purposes

And God said unto them... Have dominion over every
living thing that moveth upon the earth.
Genesis 1:28

Two planks traverse the girders.
We have aimed our wheels at them
before we see the challenger,
and begin our crossing. Resolutely,
he advances too, head down,
a dark ball rolling side to side.
He could easily give way
to leap from beam to beam,

but porcupines do not leap well.
At last he turns and waddles back,
showing us his paws' pale pads.
I honk to hasten his retreat,
a trivial affront. He halts
and bristles like a jumbo urchin,
a terrestrial oxymoron,
spiny tail buffeting the air,

while we discuss the likelihood
that quills could puncture tires.
Point made, he moves along
with all remaining dignity,
shambling at the bridgehead
into buckthorn and thimbleberry.
We pursue our casual quest
for other quasi-victories.

Lac des Deux Montagnes

Between our village here,
and distant Kanesatake
(do you see the church?)
two ferries meet midway,
three times an hour.
and haven't collided yet.

That church has witnessed —
through three centuries
since the black-skirts came —
to the Faith, and for a peace
that might obtain between
First Nations and the Last.

We, the Last, conspire to build
our golf and country club
on confiscated sacred land,
at peace among ourselves,
but in shotgun range
of the First to settle there.

Second Horse of the Apocalypse

*"And there came another horse, bright red, its rider empowered to take peace from
the earth."*
from Revelation 6:1-8.

I have climbed this summer field
so often, to its sunny summit,
reminded only rarely of its horror,
while the meadow bloomed as always —
buttercup and Queen Anne's lace,
purple vetch and hawkweed.
But now arrives November.

At the bottom, dead leaves gather
in sodden heaps, with rubbish
left by after-season tourists. They
have heard the battle rattling in
the limbs of naked trees, and
turned their backs. Three horses,
white, black and palomino,

join a wild bay mare, abetting
conquest, war and murder,
such pragmatic union useful to
their diabolic purpose. Riders
in Prussian helmets goggle back,
repossessing former glory,
mindless of artifacts broken

under hammer-hooves and strewn
in bloody pools. My eyes cast down,
and now I see in the water darkly

their reflections thundering into
imminent oblivion. To walk in
radiant fields of flowers again,
must we forget?

Peace in Our Time

"Peace is merely the desolation left behind
after the decisive operations of merciless power."
Tacitus

Leave behind at last the outrage
of that bloody winter. Glide with me
through silence whitened
by a merest sliver of a moon
behind a filigree that clutches
snow and sky. Stand atop a prairie
fallowed for the vile duration.

Scan the empty flat horizon.
Search among the circling stars.
Unhampered by substantial war,
now you have time again to shape
a fresh desire, a new distrust,
a favourite animosity, or such
another base abstraction.

Getting the Finger

As sure as rolling seasons,
hot and cold, leaf fall, comfort
of snow and greening spring,
partisan elections are coming,
Oscars, competitions and debates,
revivals, parliaments and
councils of disputing nations,

all occasions where charisma
counts. In undistinguished actors
it can swell box-office sales
to squealing fans. Preachers
having it inspire deluded faith,
and politicians rely on it to render
voters purblind and amnesiac.

As sure as creeping glaciers,
regrettable as stealthy frost,
it searches out the G-spot
of every promising affinity,
evoking wanton rapture
in defenseless individuals
and simpleminded multitudes.

Catch-22, for we are safe
from such seduction only
in chaste and cloistered solitude,
withdrawn from flesh and blood,
from legislature, church,
and all imperfect institutions
we have built for our protection.

Dada Prospective

I've moved — bed, books and shot glass
into another 'ism. I look about, and see
a Dali pocket-watch that doesn't wilt

jolly nuns from Hieronymus Bosch
streaking nude and camel-back
across the thirsty Wadi Rum

icicles dripping from a burning church
with gearhead rock wall-papering
by Bachman-Turner Overdrive —

artists should not be asked
to justify themselves but I persist
and they confess the manifest futility

of juxtaposing objects taken out of
disparate domains (inverted urinal
ten feet above the courthouse floor)

they shrug, they say old thresholds
do not admit contemporary angst
and I had best get used to living here

Left of Centre

He listens, and he speaks,
but a winter gale in the pine tops
and the clamour of unruly crows
stifle the urgent whisper
of small life on the forest floor.
Though he is a minority of one,
the rulers of the landscape
fear the dreary masses
who believe that he's a prophet.

They don't serve unless the system
gratifies their gross cupidity.
He cannot remedy that wrong.
Some, who tried, collapsed
ahead of him. He stumbles
on their bodies only half decayed
and breathing the stink of death.

The honest wielder of the axe
is worthy as the timber baron,
but captaincy is not intuitive.
He engages an elusive grace
but survives no better than those
who do without it altogether,
a dubious spirit no more
than anodyne to stress or frailty.

Still he stands and listens
through the martial measure
of bleak November's drums
for clues to his direction.
He hears no invitation
in the forest corridors,
nor comfort in the noisy hustings
on the last days of election.

Nine Eleven

1. 11 September 2001

I drive from Ottawa to Montreal
one fine clear morning,
two hours with the radio off,
in an outer space of my creation.
The road bypasses every town.

Here are flat and fenceless farms,
with silo clusters standing tall
and safely stowed with corn.
As I cross the shining river,
Monteregian hills, with towers
and temples, rise on the horizon.

Later, over and over, I am shown
the apocalypse I missed. I mute
the commentator's quavering voice,
jealous for my careless peace,
stolen in the impact of that moment.

2. 11 September 2011

Ten years on,
Ground Zero today
in the valley a big apple
orchard, laid waste
by a rogue tornado.

Stunned, still the people
come by force of
autumn Sunday habit,
to pick for themselves
through an acre of footprint.

Fruit lies bruised
among tumbled limbs.
Little remains to be gleaned,
and I make cider from windfalls
doomed to be deer bait.

Winter Reigns

Dawn doesn't break, it bends,
to a pewter shade of icy black.
Pines and spruces hiss and rattle.
Glazed and naked maples quake.
Inside the cedars, sparrows prattle.

The halfway hazard of December
finds the sleeping city unprepared.
Commuters hunched in tired surrender
crunch across the crust to cars
and set out risking fender-benders.

So Sing We Noël

Boutiques and bars, cafés and gift emporia
invite us in from snowy wastes
and parking lots

to sing good cheer along the aisles of merchandise,
because our canticles inspire
the clientele

to purchase togs and toys, furniture and finery
and candy canes... And so we carol Hodie
(this day, of all days)

Christus natus est, Allelujah! (or other
words to that effect in both
official languages.)

Order of Service

The congregation will please
observe the Sunday bulletin.
Rise (as you are able) and sing,
then sit and read the passages
prescribed and printed out in bold.

Abide the weekly lectionary readings
from both testaments, old and older,
our appeals for godly intervention,
and a homily of appropriate length.
Leave your offering in the plate.

Come forth by rows to have
the sacramental elements
(returning by the other aisle.)
Keep moving. Do not not pause
to hear a still small voice.

After the benediction and Amen
you may, if you wish, withdraw,
quietly, during the organ postlude.
Please take the bulletin with you.
There's tea or coffee in the hall.

The Source

I lift my eyes to Grasshopper Hill
where every day, year round,
neighbours bring their dogs to run
and share in warm fraternity,
both canine and humane;

where parents bring their children
to play at ball in summer, slide
or make snow angels in the winter,
kindling a collective of goodwill
that carries home with them.

More than tidy stringencies
or homiletic stipulations from
a sanctuary pulpit, such harmony
is my assurance of things hoped for,
my conviction of things not seen.

Ottawa, Canada

Hic Sedeo et Lego

I envy mediaeval monks their chance
to walk in solitary cloistered bowers,
and read from breviary, Book of Hours,
or Testament — a consecrated dance
between the spirit and the intellect,
a virtuous stewardship of precious time
from prayerful Matins to the hour of Prime

when on our vast Creation they reflect.
This afternoon, in scarf and Tilley hat
I quit my sheltered house and cosy hearth
to face October's sunny chill instead;
I found a plastic garden chair and sat.
Without a colonnade around my garth,
I did not ambulate. I simply read.

I and Thou, Martin Buber

The snow will come again,
white, cold and carried
on the wind that even now
sighs through hemlocks
rising in the darkness.

Even imaginary objects
immanate the limits
fixed by their conjurors,
rightly or wrongly, like
blind men and an elephant.

I imagine space and time,
space transparent and
essential as the air.
My moment punctuates
the endless timescape.

I am not defined. Small faith
outreaches my restricted grasp.
You grant me grace to catch
a transient glimpse beyond
a brief reflection in the void.

But snow will come again,
white, cold and carried
on the wind that even now
sighs through hemlocks
rising in the darkness.

The One-on-One Cycle

Mons Veneris

I'm not useless yet — been here before,
but the virgin camouflage, white and cold
in early morning light, has me mystified,
and I'm the first bushwhacker to the site.

There is a way. I search a stupid hour
before I find the opening that never freezes,
not a secret, but obscure for good or ill,
through the knotty tangle to the mire.

Later I take a mental memo, here recorded:
once I pass the "No Trespassing" sign and
reach the winter heartland, I must strike
along that open freshet till the cattails part.

A Word to George Herbert

Love bade me welcome, yet my soul drew back,
Guilty of dust and sin

from 'Love', George Herbert, d.1633.

The guilty sin is not in dust
that rises from your wasteland
in a scourge of sudden scruple,
like a plague of god-sent locusts
westbound on a tropic wind.

Guilt seeks excuses for audacity
in fireworks of chrysanthemum
and reckless guarantees of love.
Here is the acid test, if you pay heed
to auguries of alchemy or creed:

Love is neither gratified nor troubled
by untimely consummation;
Love yearns to offer welcome,
once the urgent leg is over and
the carnal appetite is surfeited.

December in short sleeves

if the market is closed
I sleep
on any offer

a night bird that sings briefly
and moves on
must be followed

purblind in a dark city
I see
as well as the next man

a candle lit by one
serves better
if held by another

given a single blanket
two bodies
sleep warmer than one alone

***

at cold midday
an observant publican pours
Irish mist for both,

two hard chocolates
set together
for a moment in the sun

fish and chips

at a table with no prospect
of the lochside quay —
only of a micro skirt
perched on a tall stool opposite
talking on a cell and chewing
while she finishes her beer

a pimply skinhead
drops his bike
against the window
feints a mating dance
with a rhinestone navel
in Britney hip-huggers

a pageboy blonde in slack suit
guards her carry-all
two balding men in khaki
thirty-nine and holding
watch

in one unguarded moment
the waitress, earrings dangling
winks at me unmasked
her eyes no longer focussed
on a point somewhere between
the tables and the clock.

Atelier of a Defeated Artist

In Memory of Laurie Walker, Montreal 1962-2011

Was there a path from frailty,
adolescence brittle as glass,
to mettle and brass?

from petals and wings
to timbers and welds,
to arrows and slings?

More thwarted than she knew,
her concepts grew;
her forces failed,

the fabric she left
too large to be kept,
summarily scrapped.

Si monumentum requires,
circumspice — charcoal scrawls
on chalky walls.

Parable of the Birds

A yellow warbler pauses briefly
on the sunny attic windowsill
beside her bed. "Nest here!"
exclaims Miss Phoebe, "far above
ovivorous reptiles, predatory vermin,
and cowbirds laying alien eggs."

The gurney can't negotiate
the narrow staircase to her room.
A paramedic carries her down;
she accuses him of touching her,
and he is taken into custody
for aggravated usefulness.

His wife, his parish priest,
his union steward visit him.
Not one believes he's guilty
of a crime, a misdemeanour,
even an omission. Witnesses
have taken issue with the charge.

Birds, caged or feral, at their end
are unaware and always innocent.
Safe in palliative succor, far above
ovivorous reptiles, predatory vermin,
and cowbirds laying alien eggs,
still Miss Phoebe cries, "Nest here!"

Velcrophobia

Parting is such
a rip-off.
I want you,
at arms length

Three-Part Inventions

Happy in unfallen love, and ushered
to an old cathedral choir stall
three metres from the keyboard
of her Fazioli concert grand, I have
a chambered Bach recital to myself.
How could I not be captivated!

Her dark left-hand arpeggios
in the "E-flat major" pause
for ornamental interjections
from the right. The huge "F-minor"
would have suited Franz Liszt best,
but her small hands accomplish it.

She falters and begins the lyrical
"F-major" once again, distracted
when a brash best boy retrieves
a microphone he'd set aside
beneath the massive instrument,
a major third to blight my liaison.

I hear her murmur, "Sorry! —
this should not have happened."
Lovers need not say "I'm sorry,"
but with fond intent, they do.
The passionate inventions linger
and continue, resolute and pure.

for Angela Hewitt, 7 May 2011

Nightfall, Outer Banks.

We take our February road,
from Nag's Head to Hatteras.
Vacant bungalows with widows' walks
and dark verandahs hulk on the dunes
as far to seaward as they dare.
Pilings bear them high, above
the vagaries of uncertain seas.

Broom and jessamine give way
to poverty grass and blowing sand.
Along the tide line empty shells,
perforated by the moon snail
crunch beneath our feet, ill-fated few
of legions living out of sight
below the heaving wilderness.

Hand in hand we cross the narrow neck.
Behind the barrier islands, quiet water
borrows glints of sky light, green
and muddy rose. Docks and jetties
stretch beyond plum-coloured flats.
Lazy pelicans quarrel over fish guts
tossed out from a cleaners' bench.

Banked across the flaxen sky,
ranks of clouds converge
on a hot sun dropping into
cold Pamlico Sound. The earth
turns toward a full moon rising
out of the Atlantic, and I to you,
my lambent evening star.

Faulkner's Island

Hot for any exertion,
but I have agreed
to helm the dinghy,

boom too low to duck
when going about, jib sheets
slack on either tack,

my mate more ornamental
on the foredeck
than useful in the cockpit.

After an hour in irons,
we're moored at last,
sails struck and stowed.

We strip to swim, but sprawl
face up on the dock, too tired
to fall into the tepid lake.

A warm wind roars in old pines
splayed overhead in
pallid sky and white-hot sun.

O! for the promised rain!
We will swim in the night air,
cool as two feet under.

The Circumnavigation Cycle

When I am a Loon

I swim in black, my only ornament
a white cravat, presentable
in company of upright reeds,
blue flags and cardinal flowers.
I cross the peaks and valleys
of my element, without a fear.
I am their part and partner.

When I am a loon
I swim in silence, or I sing
of signs of weather and the times.
Oblivious to all intruders,
I deride the pontooned party boats
that crawl from bay to bay,
transports of ephemeral delight.

When I am a loon,
and ice excludes me, then
I lead my children into
open estuaries by the sea,
return in spring
to air and water, sunshine,
and my patch of earth.

Summer Thunder

In Algonquin — wary and wet,
I paddle hard for the portage,
a long walk under my canoe,
or at day's end, a small tent,
and bannock over a reluctant fire.
On the road home, raindrops
bounce like flowers of evil.
Tires plane on the glassy pavement,
wipers beat, barely coping,
and I peer through spindrift
from looming semitrailers.

In the city — dry as ledgerbooks,
I watch in doubtful safety
from a glass tower, swaying
in electric cumulo-nimbus.
Commuting rain-struck
in sodden shoes or on a bike
that sprays my hunkered back,
I wish myself beneath my
solitary roaring roof, behind
rain-rattled windows, safe as
a squirrel in the scantlings.

Above Third Canyon

Whether to a woman or a river,
never an oblique approach —
I plough straight on and harmless
through Nahanni's standing waves.
My only lover sings against
the belly of my sturdy shell.

I camp on stones. My yellow tent,
my red canoe and I make up
the mandatory miniature
of colour in this painting,
insignificant by big water,
bigger talus, open scree

spruced up in velvet
or comforted by aspens on the bank.
Across the river, water roars
beneath an overhanging rock,
like traffic on a distant motorway.
The evening sun discovers

mountains sculptured in relief
against the slanting shadows.
Mountain avens, gone to seed
like dandelion clocks, a crowd
of other hoary-headed elders,
nod and tremble in the wind.

Virginia Falls

Here sunlight penetrates the canopy,
and hardy Labrador tea abounds.
Tonight our Slavey guide, Raquel,
boils a pot of it beside our supper fire,
and adds a twisted root of licorice fern.

Sweet and spicy... We suggest
this resource ought to be exploited
to benefit the local band.
It should be packaged here and sold
throughout the thirsty waiting world.

Raquel shakes her head. She says
it isn't ours, it is the earth's,
free to everyone, for scurvy
or a rash, sore throat or cough,
or adding spice to muskox.

She throws a broken twig of it
beyond our little ring of light,
dismissing an unworthy spirit.

Swann Point on the Liard

Across the ponderous river
a strip of slip supports
a cottonwood horizon,
roots exposed — an early spate
has carved and carried off the fallen.

A flux of crackle clay
and sun-baked biscuit
backs on the thicket.
Bison and bear pass by and stare
at our camp above the litter line.

Petroglyph Beach

Solitary here, I thought,
between the razorback of
snowy ramparts opposite
the place I've chosen,
and old-growth forest
dark and close to shore —

here I can explore.
I find a bird in stone,
held captive eons past,
its flight appropriated, the sun
secreted under its wing,
Promethean fire.

A woman in buckskin
walks the shingle,
heedless of me
as of the breeze
that lifts the black hair
from her shoulders.

Close around her play
her naked children.
The sempiternal dog
insists that I should throw
a ball, a solar emblem
he has offered at my feet.

Wrangell, Alaska, 6 June 2011.

The View from Thirty Thousand Feet

The land lies freshly whitened
by the blizzard yesterday. We fly
above it through a constant dusk,
keeping pace with a setting sun.
Dark forest interrupts, then yields
to bare and crinkled hills, profiled
by weak light from the west, a sky
still bright and blood red at the rim.

A spot of yellow light betrays a town
tucked in the oxbow of a stream, or at
a junction of two right-angled roads,
leading to (or from) the landscape's
four extremities. There people sit
at dinner, each with a reason or
a motivation that they never question,
asking only for that light and warmth.

The yardlight of a solitary farmstead
by its quarter section punctuates
the crease of gridiron laid across
the arrant randomness of streams.
They wander aimlessly, it seems,
with neither purpose nor utility,
but have in fact inspired direction --
the inevitable way to distant seas.

Voice of the Grand Canyon

Our craft descends through time,
through sleeper, tongue and eddy —
two thousand feet, two billion years

below the diamond pinnacle,
an aisle of Romanesque basilicas
and Gothic oratories, fortresses

with postern gates above the
primal and perpetual percussion,
red-walled and chalky green

beneath their looming barbicans.
Sacred datura drapes the granite
monuments to poet-prophet Zoroaster

and obsidian temples to eternal Vishnu,
spirit of primeval floods, long before
the spawning of the universe.

Ancient lizards are mute keepers
of these precincts now, among
the prickly pear and tamarisk.

Silent bighorns pause in this deep cloister,
see us pass and turn away to graze.
Only the freckled canyon wren

creeps the walls and overhangs,
pokes crevices for mites and insects,
seeks cooling shade by water,

gathers webs and lichens
for her nest, and sings a loud
and long descending song.

Motown Layover

Three time zones east of yesterday,
still I rise early. A pale moon fails.
I find a coffee, walk the vacant streets.
The horizon of an ailing city
rises out of ashes, dark against
a glowing sky of blood and roses.

A carrion crow relieves the owl of
its night watch of my wakeful hours.
High-spirited Sunday sparrows,
starlings, larks and winter finches
forage in the gutters; no other life.

This cruel cold may cauterize
two years of weeping lesions.
I fly before the dirty weather strikes.

Detroit, 20 February 2011

Drake Passage

Beyond the Horn, four centuries
after Francis in the Golden Hind,
there follow us across the Snake
the giant petrels of his logbook
and a black-browed albatross
spanning seven feet of wind.

The taffrail mounts and falls again
against the constant boundary
that from the second day of Genesis
has separated sea from sky.

I usually paddle a canoe, shorter than
the wavelength of these uneasy seas.
Our space-ship, bearing south-south-east
orbits another world. The circling sun
breaks through the overcast,
dropping rainbows in the sea
and gleaming on a virgin shore.

Fiji in September

Seasons overlap, like these hills
folding up and away from the sea,
flickering and flexible in the haze.
Blossoms blaze on trees
still heavy with their fruit,
and spring flowers rise
among the elevated tassels
of February's grasses.

The rim of the blinding sea
frets against the coral a mile away.
Shallows slap the nearer beach
of broken molluscs and crustaceans,
of granulated mountains.
The sun stands high in the north,
its white heat pounding through
a gaping fissure in the ozone.

I climb past coco palms,
through banyan and mahogany
hung with strangler figs and orchids,
turning at last to stare across the canopy.
A further path to greater heights is clear,
but first it drops below the eminence
that I have reached, and this
is far and high enough.

Silk Road

We set out for the Gobi,
believing we're prepared.
The Silk Road, artery
from the heart of China,
has defeated others,
and we take our safeguards,
antidotes for western frailties —
antiseptics, analgesics,
anodynes and soporifics...

We will progress, we think,
between our air-conditioned
five-star caravanseries
in air-conditioned transport,
carrying our bottled water,
squeezing China into twenty days...

two long-noses in a load
of Cantonese Canadian
unilingual anglophones
looking for their roots –
in the dark since Friday
in Toronto. We've crossed the Line,
and suddenly it's Sunday in Hong Kong.
An empty terminal — children join us,
fifth grade from the Grammar School,
in pink-checked shirts and frocks,
— a field trip to the Wall —
and western mandarins
with cell phones in their hands,
joint ventures in attaché cases,
and the morning in their eyes.

We drop from the sun
into daub and wattle, air-conditioned
since another alien ruler, Genghis Khan,
open to outer space.
Beyond the yellow ribbons,
houseflies and small red taxicabs.
A tour guide toting shoulder bag
and bottled water gathers her chicks.
The café waitress, precarious
on platform soles, leans on the counter,
picking her teeth.

Two TVs entertain a nursing mother.
Husband, head thrown back, snores gently
near the porcelain spittoon.
A lost American in open shirt
shouts at his cell phone,
clutches his boarding pass,
watches the board
as his flight creeps up,
and reaching deadline,
slices into desert dust
above a Bank of China
billboard caligraphed in English.

At the end of the Wall, we follow
Marco Polo through the Jaiyu Gate.
Towers of the Tang
and snow-capped mountains
watch the ancient Corridor.
Counterfeit pools reflect the heat,
but these hand-made plots
of winter wheat and early corn
are watered by the snows of Qilian.

White goats and Bactrian camels
forage in the sagebrush suburbs.
Wind farms fan the gray air.
Shacks and stacks of alien enterprise
stand in the haze on a false
horizon under distant peaks.
Any man with a shovel works -
clearing ditches, building dikes,
loading and unloading camel dung.
With a motor-trike he can become
a cabby or a one-horse teamster.

Sparse green ribbons lead us
under hills of dwarf red willow,
by nameless bivouacs of felt and lattice.
Kazak herders welcome us at last,
ignorant of whatever demagogue
in Beijing, far to the east,
now imagines that he rules.

Xinjiang Autonomous Region, May 2000

Sas-Bahu

In a valley of the Aravili foothills,
Lake Baghela shines in winter sun.
Across the water from the dusty road,
have stood for a millennium
two sandstone temples,
"Mother" and her "Daughter-in-Law,"
once vandalized by Moghul raiders, now
by poachers hunting souvenirs —

but still, in flourishing geometry
remains a decorous pavilion,
portaled in the four directions,
pillared with a deep relief where
minor deities and nymphets rut and frolic.

Here Lord Shiva the Transmuter
meditates in manifold apotheoses.
There an empty cell awaits
the coming of Lord Vishnu,
Second Person of the Trinity,
preserver of the universe, governor
and spirit of all time and being.

In the meantime, human life persists.
Below the ruined Mewar fortresses,
on steps of a ramparted ghat
a modest woman in a sari washes clothes,
and gleaming boys are bathing.

November, Golan Heights

We moved the spiderwort
indoors, to a sunny window.

Hard frost last night; today
we uproot and throw away
all the other alien plants,
overseen through summer
by a coterie of dreamers —

marigolds and sweet potato,
lobelia, mums and fuchsia,
coleus, and Swedish ivy.
Turn the earth for April,
scrub the grubby tools —

out of animus, or onus....
Now we mark the naked trees
awaiting the numb comfort
of unforgiving snow
falling heavy at their roots.

Dislocations

Luxor, half an hour after dawn.
I weigh the chance that brought me here,
before the day begins. No horse's hooves
rattle the Corniche, no motor horns,
no country-and-eastern from the tour boats
on the Nile. Silence by the cold fires
on the river-wall where boatmen
make their tea each evening. Across the river,
neither camel gripe nor yelping hounds,
not even crickets — no night sounds.

My final waking is a breaking string,
and a throb that lingers into nothing —
one low strain, while Luxor slumbers on.
But I have heard black Memnon
moaning in the lonely barrens.
Mute for centuries until today, his colossus
rises tall beyond the river — not the Trojan hero,
King of Ethiopia, but Pharaoh Amen-hotep III,
who every dawning faces his indifferent deity
and mourns the splendour of old Thebes.

Reading at the Cafe Eklektika

I have led you to a wall. Will you now
complete the following questionnaire?
        How high is it?
(Check one of the following) Is it built
        of brick?
        of stone?
        of stucco?
        other? (specify)
Are you inside or out?
What's on the other side?
Do you care? (Choose one)
        yes
        no
It's up to me to make you care.
May I have a glass of water?

It is my wall, after all,
and though you wonder
what's beyond it, I won't tell.
I'll spread you out beside me
against its sheltered side,
an espaliered pear in winter,
anchored to the yellow bricks
(did you imagine they were red?)
where children (any children —
you may insert your own)
climb our contorted limbs
to open inconvenient shutters.

Is the picture clearer now? My wall's
a straight space, never curved,
and it extends forever.
Not what you had in mind, perhaps, but
the children have discovered windows.
What shall I add ? — the sound of snow,
large flakes on weary wings,
melting into tongues against the glass.

Budapest, June 2000

Clam Diggers

Sunset on a winter day, the low-tide marsh
a silver marker crossing the mist, all else
reduced to silhouettes against the sky and water.
Essentials only -- sun a red ball tangled
in the branches of a gum tree,
a creature as deciduous as ourselves.

Salt floods and beetles collaborate to kill
the barrier island pines. Trunks and limbs
rise naked now above new growth,
lofty lookouts, roosts for hawks
red-tailed and sharp-shinned,
preying on endangered species.

Clam diggers, grubbing the mud
in the rosy light, bow like commas,
each a hesitation in the text
of the apocalypse. A snowy egret
lopes across the winter sedges,
unconscious of impending poetry.

Outport

A herring gull flies into the overcast
and drops a shell, again and again. Low tide
exposes mussel-laden pilings, fucoid rocks,
stone-filled cribs, and jointed conduits
that drain the outport's main cloaca to the sea.
At the harbour mouth the north Atlantic
boils across the white-hot shoals.

Old cottages and sturdy sheds
survive below a bald declivity
that backs the mother village,
but beyond it, drills and dynamite
and back-hoes break the rock
for dormitory streets and homes
to overlook the basin and the sea.

No cruisers in the winter slips, no tourists
or their keepers; our own folk only, crews —
on tugs, on pilot boats, on tough Cape Islanders,
on a beetling ferry, unlikely shape of ship
but harbour-worthy, and on rusty
coast guard vessels grounded and careened
for scaling and repainting sanguinary red.

The fogbank and the prospect clear.
Morning paints the April shore
with pigments of October; a pine,
its low limbs dead and dropping,
lofts a green and tufted spire,
and naked trees of summer shiver
in a rosy cloud of swollen buds.

Nova Scotia, 2003

Mader's Wharf

On winter's shortest day, we loop
the Aspotogan shore, stopping
by a snowbound shingle cottage,
yellow shed and polychrome
cape islanders. We ask about the
floating trays of seedling oysters,
three full years from shucking, but
no one volunteers to answer.

Do we care if nothing's said, or done?
Down the shore we sit with local folk
for chowder, beer and a baguette.
Beyond the warmth of Mader's Wharf
Mahone Bay lies, hove to, beneath the ice.
Three churches scan the empty cove
for all denominations of delinquency --
established or dissenting or heretical,
while in slack water, still and slow,
we trust the tide to ebb and flow.

Crossing New Brunswick, 2010

The new-cut highway
opens up the second growth,
exposing naked aspens,
tall and trembling, foliage
covering just their heads,
like gangly prepubescent
adolescents discovered sharing
showers at a summer camp.

We penetrate their private parts,
where deer, bobcat and weasel,
hawk and jay, and other denizens
annoyed by this intrusion,
jealous of obscurity, retreat.

Ravishing becomes an act of love,
the thoroughfare the only way.
We drive ahead, submissive
to our fortune, leaving it behind us
for our children and all those
who fall into their altered places,
forgetful of our passing
as soon as we are gone.

Nightfall, Mississippi Mills

Stone shells stand empty, after decades
of decay. One turbine roars, to light
a dormitory town. One bright window
shines on floes of foam, scudding
from the tailrace of the last cascade.

With urban currency we buy our light
from country rivers. This town might
have made a city once, on promises
of other years, but all the forest
is used up, and the soil too thin.

Night strikes. Our habitat contracts
into this inner space. Distant lights
cast wavering trails across the race
to where it slides beneath the ice.

Eagle Lake

The cottage flag lifts in the drift
of morning air. Like a flaming sword,
the early sun casts a blaze
of antique gold on the pewter lake.
The far shore inverts in its shadow.

White gulls hover over deep reflections,
shrilling like boys, rash and impatient
with gravity and tribal boundary
exulting in opening day at camp.
Chickadees announce themselves

by name, and chip for pine nuts
in the yearling cones. I watch the lake
through aging pines. They are dying.
Oak and cedar take their place.
For forty years we've seen it coming;

forty more will end the succession.
We do not change. Somewhere
a freight train threads the bush,
its wailing voice alerting no one
at an empty level crossing.

Rock Harlequin

A morning fog pours down the portage
up to Spectacle, like unbidden doubt.
A dragonfly scoops the last mosquitoes.
Ravens, jays, woodpeckers cry alarm —
and then the plaintive nuthatch,
lofty twitter of retreating warblers,
gossip of chickadees. A pair of loons
begin their counterpoint of fear.

In a rocky seam pale corydalis blooms,
rising from the ashen grit of lichens.
Dry leaves curl and ride the pool's
invisible mantle, early outcasts of September.
Out of the depth lift ghostly deadheads.
Water shield springs up on coiling threads,
and three-square sedge reflects and bends
at curious angles. I am the curiosity.

The first breeze scatters fragments
of the sky across the bay. Marbled foam
washes the shallows. The outer lake
turns silver, flecked with shadows
of the dark shore opposite. Silhouettes
of pickerel weed stand up against it
like the horn-beaked heads of old fathers
remarking the redemption of the prodigal.

About the author

Born in Toronto, E. Russell Smith was educated at the University of Toronto Schools and McGill University (M.Sc.). He married Barbara Emms of Montreal in 1955. After a period of casting about for a suitable career, he was forced by impending fatherhood in 1958 to settle on teaching high school in Wingham, Ont. This turned out to be a serendipitous move, as teaching suited him, and he suited teaching.

After two years and the birth of two daughters, Terry and Allison, the family moved to Ottawa where they have been more or less continuously ever since. A son, Greg, arrived in 1965. When Russ left teaching in 1988, he had been the Head of Science at Gloucester High School for 25 years.

A turning point in his life had occurred, however, in 1970-71, when the family spent a sabbatical year at Cambridge University. Ostensibly studying history of art, Russ was to discover during this year a bent toward creative writing. Back in Ottawa, he proceeded toward an M.A. in English (1983) at the University of Ottawa.

Russ finally left teaching in order to write full time. Previously he had published a considerable body of technical material, mostly on contract, but thenceforth his efforts were to be directed chiefly toward fiction and poetry.

They liked to travel in the spring and fall, and enjoy Ottawa's winter and summer delights. They explored Europe and the Middle East as far as Egypt, Turkey and Israel. In the other direction they penetrated China to its western extremities. In Canada they have been from Point Pelee to Cambridge Bay NWT, and from Nain Labrador to Tofino BC, traveling by car, train, bus, plane and canoe, as appropriate.

Widowed since 2002, Russ still makes frequent trips, recently in the company of Areta Crowell.

You can find Russ and links to his other published works from his website ;

http://web.ncf.ca/ab297/

About The RightEyedDeer Press

The RightEyedDeer Press is an offshoot of a global writers forum, The Write Idea. The forum is free to join and welcomes new members whether they be readers or writers. They have a supportive community and strive to improve their work.

You can find the forum at ;

http://www.helenwhittaker.net/phpBB2/index.php

The forum, through The RightEyedDeer Press, also publish a magazine, 'The RightEyedDeer' which is available approximately quarterly as either a free PDF download or alternatively in print via our Lulu storefront. Each issue contains poetry and fiction, along with showcasing a featured artist.

Also at the storefront you can buy anthologies compiled from the various competitions held through the forum.

'Petroglyph Beach' is also available through this storefront, and at the time of publishing will be available in various ebook formats too.

You can find the storefront at ;

http://www.lulu.com/spotlight/therighteyeddeer

or 'The RightEyedDeer' magazine via its own website ;

http://therighteyeddeer.weebly.com/